FUNDRAISING WORKBOOK

for Interns

Published by LearnPro Inc.
©2012 Karen Young.
ISBN 978-0-9880571-1-1
#379 - 33771 George Ferguson Way
Abbotsford, BC   Canada   V2S 2M5

Toll Free: 1-888-876-3984
info@learnpro.ca

The *Fundraising Workbook* is intended to accompany the *Fundraising Primer,* also by Karen Young, and may be filled out by Interns under the supervision of a fundraising professional.

Interns should be placed in currently active Organizations, working on real life situations that will help the Organization, as well as give the Intern valuable experience.

All Interns will complete the initial sections. Additional sections will be assigned by the Supervisor according to the following guidelines.
1. The need of the Organization for a piece of research.
2. The length of time that the Intern is available to the Organization, from one to six months.
3. The interests and general skills of the Intern.

The Workbook research activity is intended to supplement additional hands-on experiences.

The work that results from this Internship may result in a final report that can be graded.

Fundraising Workbook for Interns

Instructions to the Development Intern

Each Intern should complete the preliminary Groundwork.
Additional Sections to be completed will be assigned by your Supervisor, and will vary according to
- The requirements of the Organization
- The Intern - interests, field of study, career goals
- The time available for the Internship

Assigned
☒ Groundwork (all)
☒ Ethics (all)
☒ Preparation (all)

☐ Identifying the Need
☐ Partnerships
☐ Donor Development
☐ Grants
☐ Events Management
☐ Communications
☐ Volunteer Management
☐ Social Enterprise

Additional tasks may be assigned to Interns as required, and may include
☐ Data entry
☐ File management
☐ General office duties

Supervisor: _____

Fundraising Workbook

Contents

Groundwork	7
Ethics	9
Preparation	11
Identifying Need	15
Donor Relations	27
Research	31
Grants	35
Events	41
Communications	57
Volunteer Management	61
Social Enterprise	67

NOTES

Groundwork

Resource Development is the activity of increasing donations of cash or necessary goods or services for a Nonprofit Organization. These resource-generating skills are of benefit to Nonprofits and can also be applied to business ventures.

Preparation is essential and is the key to success. Study to gain a thorough understanding of the Organization, and of your role in it. To conduct research, connect directly with people, ask questions and build relationships. This is a core activity, and expected during these studies.

Additional research may be done online at the Association of Fundraising Professionals website.

Define the following

Charity

_____

_____

_____

Nonprofit (Society; Organization; NGO)

_____

_____

Social Enterprise

_____

_____

Legal requirements

Nonprofits are obligated to report their activities and financial standing to several audiences.
Who does a Nonprofit Organization report to, and what do they report?

_____	_____
_____	_____
_____	_____
_____	_____

© Karen Young. 2012.

NOTES

What is the year end report called, and what is included in it?
_____
_____

When is it appropriate to issue a tax receipt?
_____
_____

When is it not permitted to issue a tax receipt?
_____
_____
_____

Are there exceptions? If so, describe them.
_____
_____

Ethics

Describe the ethics of these situations.

Paying a Fundraising professional.
Fees may be paid based on_____
_____

Fees may not be paid based on _____
_____

Allocating donations that have been Directed.
_____
_____

© Karen Young. 2012.

NOTES

Preparation

Answer the following based on your Intership host.
Describe the Mandate of the Organization in your own words.

_____

_____

_____

_____

Describe the Mission and Vision of the Organization, and explain.

_____

_____

_____

_____

_____

_____

Identify the people, by name, in each category that the Resource Development staff might work with. Describe each person's field of influence.

Board members

_____

_____

_____

_____

_____

_____

_____

NOTES

Frontline Staff
_____
_____
_____
_____
_____
_____

Volunteers (key volunteers)
_____
_____
_____
_____

Other
_____
_____
_____

NOTES

Identifying Need

Find/create/explore five projects that require Development.
Meet with the people identified in the previous section and ask for their ideas.

1. _____
2. _____
3. _____
4. _____
5. _____

Research similar organizations for Projects that may be adapted.

_____
_____
_____

PROJECT SAMPLE: Description *Health Fair for neighbourhood*

Human Resources: __12__ Number of People   ❑ highly skilled   ☒ workers
Timeline to plan: __3__ Days (Weeks) Months   Timeline to implement __2__ Days (Weeks) Months

Expense
❑ Rent $__25__ ❑ Staff $__225__ ❑ Supplies $__100__ ❑ Other $____ (explain) _____

What is the expected return?
❑ Cash $____   ☒ Public relations   ❑ Other _____

What is the cost to develop?

SAMPLE PROJECT DESCRIPTION	# People	# Hours	$$ Expense
Advertising (volunteers word of mouth)	3	25	
Printing			25
Table rental			25
Phone calls to arrange	5	10	
Refreshments and samples			75
Staff paid to oversee the project			225

© Karen Young. 2012.

NOTES

PROJECT ONE: Description _____

Human Resources: _____Number of People   ❏ skilled   ❏ directed workers
Timeline to plan: _____ Days Weeks Months   Timeline to implement ____ Days Weeks Months

Expense
❏ Rent $____   ❏ Staff $____   ❏ Supplies $____   ❏ Other $____ (explain) _____

What is the expected return?
❏ Cash $____   ❏ Public relations   ❏ Other _____

What is the cost to develop?

PROJECT ONE DESCRIPTION	# People	# Hours	$$ Expense

PROJECT TWO: Description _____

Human Resources: _____Number of People   ❏ skilled   ❏ directed workers
Timeline to plan: _____ Days Weeks Months   Timeline to implement ____ Days Weeks Months

Expense
❏ Rent $____   ❏ Staff $____   ❏ Supplies $____   ❏ Other $____ (explain) _____

Expected Return
❏ Cash $____   ❏ Public relations   ❏ Other _____

What is the cost to develop?

PROJECT TWO DESCRIPTION	# People	# Hours	$$ Expense

© Karen Young. 2012.

NOTES

PROJECT THREE: Description _____

Human Resources: _____ Number of People   ❑ skilled   ❑ directed workers
Timeline to plan: _____ Days Weeks Months   Timeline to implement _____ Days Weeks Months

Expense
❑ Rent $____   ❑ Staff $____   ❑ Supplies $____   ❑ Other $____ (explain) _____

What is the expected return?
❑ Cash $____   ❑ Public relations   ❑ Other _____

What is the cost to develop?

PROJECT THREE DESCRIPTION	# People	# Hours	$$ Expense

PROJECT FOUR: Description _____

Human Resources: _____ Number of People   ❑ skilled   ❑ directed workers
Timeline to plan: _____ Days Weeks Months   Timeline to implement _____ Days Weeks Months

Expense
❑ Rent $____   ❑ Staff $____   ❑ Supplies $____   ❑ Other $____ (explain) _____

What is the expected return?
❑ Cash $____   ❑ Public relations   ❑ Other _____

What is the cost to develop?

PROJECT FOUR DESCRIPTION	# People	# Hours	$$ Expense

© Karen Young. 2012.

NOTES

PROJECT FIVE: Description _____

Human Resources: _____ Number of People ❑ skilled ❑ directed workers
Timeline to plan: _____ Days Weeks Months Timeline to implement _____ Days Weeks Months

Expense
❑ Rent $____ ❑ Staff $____ ❑ Supplies $____ ❑ Other $____ (explain) _____

What is the expected return?
❑ Cash $____ ❑ Public relations ❑ Other _____

What is the cost to develop?

PROJECT FIVE DESCRIPTION	# People	# Hours	$$ Expense

Based on the analysis of expense and expected return, which project or projects do you recommend?
_____
_____
_____

Defend this position.
_____
_____
_____
_____
_____

NOTES

Partnerships

Formal or informal alliances may be formed to benefit all. Identify several specific examples, below.

1. Sister Agencies (near or different region) _____

2. Competitive Agencies _____

3. Community Groups _____

4. Corporations _____

5. Individuals _____

Why are these alliances or partnerships valuable?
1. _____
2. _____
3. _____
4. _____
5. _____

List potential Project Partners/Supporters (specifically)

Sister Agencies (related by different service, same or similar client)
Same region _____
_____

Outside of catchment area _____
_____

Competitive Agencies (same service, same client)
_____
_____
_____

NOTES

Community Groups
_____
_____
_____
_____
_____

Corporations
_____
_____
_____
_____
_____
_____

Individuals
_____
_____
_____
_____

Other (describe)
_____
_____
_____

NOTES

Donor Relations

Summarize annual donations, using figures from the previous two years.
(Work with the Finance Department.)

Gifts $5,000 and less

Description	# Donors	$ Total	% New
		$	

Describe five ways to encourage an increase in general giving,
1. _____
2. _____
3. _____
4. _____
5. _____

Major Gifts

Description	# Donors	$ Total	% New
		$	

Describe five ways to encourage an increase in Major Gifts giving,
1. _____
2. _____
3. _____
4. _____
5. _____

© Karen Young. 2012.

NOTES

Bequests

Description	# Donors	$ Total	% New
		$	

Bequests: Describe ways to encourage an increase in Bequests,

1. _____

2. _____

3. _____

4. _____

5. _____

In-Kind (large) gifts

Description	# Donors	$ Total	% New
		$	

Describe in-kind gifts.
❑ Food   ❑ Clothing   ❑ Furnishings   ❑ Professional Service   ❑ Other_____

In-kind (large gifts): Describe ways to encourage an increase in giving,

_____

_____

_____

Are small in-kind gifts recorded? ❑ Yes ❑ No   Are they recognized? ❑ Yes ❑ No
In-kind (small gifts): Describe ways to encourage an increase in giving,

_____

_____

© Karen Young. 2012.

NOTES

What three steps can be taken immediately to implement an increase in overall giving?

1. _____

2. _____

3. _____

Research

Identify three potential donors that have not given to this Organization in the past year.

1. _____

2. _____

3. _____

What methods were used in the research.
_____
_____

Explain why you believe that these donors may be persuaded to give.
_____
_____
_____

How can these prospective donors be asked to give? Outline the best strategy.
Compelling case _____
_____
_____

NOTES

Door Opener (supporter of the Organization who is able to make an introduction to a donor) _____

_____

_____

_____

Followup _____

_____

_____

_____

Action Step

_____

_____

NOTES

NOTES

Date Due	Funder	Amount
Description		Staff Champion

Date Due	Funder	Amount
Description		Staff Champion

Create or add the deadlines for the Letter of Inquiry and for Application to the Grants Calendar of the Organization.

Identify three potential Grants that are $50,000 or more

Date Due	Funder	Amount
Description		Staff Champion

Date Due	Funder	Amount
Description		Staff Champion

© Karen Young. 2012.

NOTES

Date Due	Funder	Amount
Description		Staff Champion

Identify three grants that are $200,000 or more that could be applied for.

Date Due	Funder	Amount
Description		Staff Champion

Date Due	Funder	Amount
Description		Staff Champion

Consult with your Supervisor about which Grant/s could be pursued.
Work with the project Champion to draft an application.

Include a budget.

DESCRIPTION	EXPENSE	INCOME

NOTES

Events

Events are held by most Nonprofit Organizations to raise money, to increase donations, to reach out to the community, and to celebrate with current supporters.

List the events that are currently undertaken by the Organization. Include all regions, and categories.

Signature fundraising event (describe)

_____

_____

_____

_____

The number of people that attended the event _____

Were funds raised? If yes:
 ❑ under $500 ❑ $501 - $1,000 ❑ $1,001 - $2,500 ❑ $2,501 - $10,000 ❑ $ more
What was the cost to the Organization to participate? (Average) $ _____

The number of person-hours were allocated to organize the event #_____

Is there a way to increase or create revenue for this event?
 ❑ Yes. Estimate increased revenue. $_____

Create a workplan to achieve this goal (use the page opposite).

Small fundraising events (describe)

_____

_____

_____

The number of people that attended the event _____

Were funds raised? If yes:
 ❑ under $500 ❑ $501 - $1,000 ❑ $1,001 - $2,500 ❑ $2,501 - $10,000 ❑ $ more
What was the cost to the Organization to participate? (Average) $ _____

The number of person-hours were allocated to organize the event #_____

© Karen Young. 2012.

NOTES

Is there a way to increase or create revenue for this event?
❏ Yes.   Estimate increased revenue. $_____

Create a workplan to achieve this goal (use the page opposite).

Third party fundraising event (Describe)
_____
_____
_____
_____

The number of people that attended the event _____

Were funds raised? If yes:
❏ under $500   ❏ $501 - $1,000   ❏ $1,001 - $2,500   ❏ $2,501 - $10,000   ❏ $ more
What was the cost to the Organization to participate? (Average) $ _____

The number of person-hours were allocated to organize the event #_____

Is there a way to increase or create revenue for this event?
❏ Yes.   Estimate increased revenue. $_____

Create a workplan to achieve this goal (use the page opposite).

© Karen Young. 2012.

NOTES

Celebration Event (describe)

_____
_____
_____

The number of people that attended the event_____

Were funds raised? If yes:
 ❏ under $500 ❏ $501 - $1,000 ❏ $1,001 - $2,500 ❏ $2,501 - $10,000 ❏ $ more
What was the cost to the Organization to participate? (Average) $ _____

The number of person-hours were allocated to organize the event #_____

Is there a way to increase or create revenue for this event?
 ❏ Yes. Estimate increased revenue. $_____

Create a workplan to achieve this goal (use the page opposite).

Recognition Event (describe)

_____
_____
_____

The number of people that attended the event _____

Were funds raised? If yes:
 ❏ under $500 ❏ $501 - $1,000 ❏ $1,001 - $2,500 ❏ $2,501 - $10,000 ❏ $ more
What was the cost to the Organization to participate? (Average) $ _____

The number of person-hours were allocated to organize the event #_____

Is there a way to increase or create revenue for this event?
 ❏ Yes. Estimate increased revenue. $_____

Create a workplan to achieve this goal (use the page opposite).

© Karen Young. 2012.

NOTES

Public Relations Event

_____

_____

_____

The number of people that attended the event_____

Were funds raised? If yes:
 ❏ under $500   ❏ $501 - $1,000   ❏ $1,001 - $2,500   ❏ $2,501 - $10,000   ❏ $ more
What was the cost to the Organization to participate? (Average) $ _____

The number of person-hours were allocated to organize the event #_____

Is there a way to increase or create revenue for this event?
 ❏ Yes.   Estimate increased revenue. $_____

Create a workplan to achieve this goal (use the page opposite).

Other Event (describe)

_____

_____

_____

_____

The number of people that attended the event_____

Were funds raised? If yes:
 ❏ under $500   ❏ $501 - $1,000   ❏ $1,001 - $2,500   ❏ $2,501 - $10,000   ❏ $ more
What was the cost to the Organization to participate? (Average) $ _____

The number of person-hours were allocated to organize the event #_____

Is there a way to increase or create revenue for this event?
 ❏ Yes.   Estimate increased revenue. $_____

Create a workplan to achieve this goal (use the page opposite).

© Karen Young. 2012.

NOTES

Is there a way to increase positive public profile from these events
❑ Yes. Please describe your thoughts in detail
Estimate the effect of increased exposure. $_____
Create a workplan to achieve this goal (use the page opposite)
_____
_____
_____
_____
_____

New Events

If creating a new event, gather the following information
Who will benefit? How will they benefit?
Clients or Members_____

Community _____

Other _____

Financial goal (or other)
   ❑ Budget $ _____   PR _____

Overview of planned event (what is it?)
Focus: ❑ Entertainment   ❑ Education   ❑ Recognition   ❑ Fundraising   ❑ Other

Vision Statement (event) _____

Describe the guest experience in five words or less _____

Refreshments _____

Entertainment/Activity _____

© Karen Young. 2012.

NOTES

Describe the event planning tasks
- ❏ Planning Committee _____
- ❏ Entertainment _____
- ❏ Refreshment _____
- ❏ Venue _____
- ❏ Media and PR _____
- ❏ Sponsorship _____
- ❏ Logistics _____
- ❏ Other _____

Steering Committee (projected) – responsible for the event

Name	Contact	Notes
____	_____	_____
____	_____	_____
____	_____	_____
____	_____	_____

Sub Committee Responsibilities
- Planning • Venue • Volunteers • Décor • Other activities
- Door Prizes • Sponsorships • Media and public relations • Registration
- Recognition for committee/organizers/donors • Financial oversight

© Karen Young. 2012.

NOTES

Fundraising Workbook for Interns

Create an Action Plan, prioritizing activities

Number of Attendees: Target _____

Planning Budget

Description	Expense	Income	Net
Venue			
Catering			
Entertainment/Activity			
Marketing			
Printing			
Sponsors			
Ticket Sales			
Donations			

Venue description
❑ Ballroom   ❑ Park   ❑ Conference Room   ❑ Other _____

❑ Power   ❑ Kitchen Facilities   ❑ Specific Amenities _____

Accommodates #_____people

Refreshments Committee Chair _____

❑ Provided   ❑ Will be purchased   ❑ Prepared by staff or volunteers

❑ Sit down meal   ❑ Passed Appetizers   ❑ Food Stations   ❑ Picnic style

Other _____

Décor
Theme _____

❑ Centre pieces   ❑ Theme decor   ❑ Other _____

© Karen Young. 2012.

NOTES

Promotion Design Committee Chair _____

Marketing Committee Chair _____

❑ Newspaper   ❑ Magazine/Trade Journal _____

❑ Email to database   ❑ Letter to Donors and Suppliers

❑ Social Media and Web   ❑ Other _____

Ticket pricing, including strategy
$_____ Single ticket $_____ Early Bird pricing $_____ Group Rates

Explain the strategy _____

Tickets selling (if applicable)
❑ Paypal   ❑ Cheque   ❑ Cash   ❑ Credit Card

❑ Website   ❑ Third Party site   ❑ Office (in person or by telephone) only

Describe why these choices were made_____
_____

Entertainment/Speakers
Describe the entertainment. _____

Research possible entertainers or speakers. Include their usual fees. _____
_____

Additional fundraising activities (describe)
❑ Raffle_____

❑ Balloon Pop_____

❑ Dunk Tank_____

❑ Other_____

How many prizes will be needed for these activities? _____

© Karen Young. 2012.

NOTES

Communications

Communications activities inform and direct the perceptions of the public-at-large — including donors and future donors — toward the Organization.

Review the Communications and Public Relations Policy of the Organization

Who is responsible for
- Emergency communications? _____

- Public relations communications? _____

What is the Key Messaging for Public Relations communications? Write it here.
_____
_____

What is the annual plan for messaging? (Annually recurring press releases, for example).
1. _____
2. _____
3. _____

Through which Channels is the Key Messaging pushed? When?
❑ Letters to supporters _____

❑ Newsletter _____

❑ Web _____

❑ Email to database _____

❑ Newspaper _____

❑ Radio _____

❑ TV _____

❑ Facebook _____

❑ Twitter_____

❑ Other _____

© Karen Young. 2012.

NOTES

Please describe gaps in messaging delivery that you observe.
_____
_____
_____
_____

Create a Press Release that fits within the Organization's PR campaign.
_____
_____
_____
_____
_____

Research a story

It must fit within the established criteria (length, focus, tone).
- Write a story, and include a Call to Action, to measure effectiveness of the Public Relations policy.
- When approved, send the story out through both established and new channels.
- Follow up to ensure story is placed.
- Measure the response.

Story of Success

_____
_____
_____
_____
_____
_____
_____

© Karen Young. 2012.

NOTES

Volunteer Management

Volunteers help fulfil the Mandate of the Organization, performing necessary tasks or expanding the public reach.

Describe the Volunteer Program
Volunteers are used for _____

_____

The barriers to operating a smooth Volunteer Program may be

❑ Limited training time   ❑ Confidentiality   ❑ Skill required   ❑ Low priority due to high workload

How can these barriers be overcome _____

_____

Describe an ideal Volunteer for this type of Program
❑ Skilled   ❑ Professional   ❑ Requires a stipend   ❑ Corporate group   ❑ One time

❑ Long term   ❑ Individual   ❑ Other _____

Benefits to the Organization of having Volunteers
_____
_____
_____

Benefits to the volunteer
_____
_____
_____

Reasons to attract Volunteers
_____
_____
_____

© Karen Young. 2012.

NOTES

Risks

_____

_____

_____

How are risks mitigated?

_____

_____

_____

Review the following documents
• Volunteer Application   • Volunteer Orientation   • Volunteer Handbook   • Volunteer Job Descriptions

Describe five ways to recruit volunteers
1. _____

2. _____

3. _____

4. _____

5. _____

Create a Volunteer Application
Include ❑ Contact information ❑ Emergency contact ❑ Special skills

Describe the Orientation of Volunteers

_____

_____

_____

© Karen Young. 2012.

NOTES

Create an Orientation Handout

Include ☐ Supervisor Name ☐ Location Address and contact ☐ Emergency Procedures

How are Volunteers evaluated?
_____
_____

How are Volunteer Statistics gathered?
_____

By whom? _____

Why? _____

Create a new Volunteer Position
Research the need, talking to staff. Write the Job Description.
_____
_____

Create an advertisement to fill the position.
_____
_____

© Karen Young. 2012.

NOTES

Social Enterprise

If the Organization does not operate a Social Enterprise, complete this section. (If the Organization does operate a Social Enterprise, this section may be skipped: continue on page 71).

Research five potentially compatible business models that could easily integrate with the Organization.
Sale of Goods _____

Provide a Service _____

Online Sales _____

Education _____

Referrals _____

Explain the reasons that they are compatible with the Organization.
_____
_____
_____
_____
_____

Cost analysis: what are the start up costs (list)?
Venue _____

Staff (and benefits) _____

Goods _____

Setup and Startup expense _____

IT _____

Inventory _____

Advertising _____

Licenses and Fees _____

© Karen Young. 2012.

NOTES

Other _____

Benefit analysis: what is the potential human return?
_____
_____

Operating analysis: what is the net benefit (financial and otherwise) in operating the suggested models?
_____
_____
_____

Create a Budget Form

DESCRIPTION	EXPENSE	INCOME

© Karen Young. 2012.

NOTES

If the Organization operates a Social Enterprise please complete this section.

Briefly describe the Enterprise.
_____

Who directly benefits from the Enterprise? In what ways?
_____
_____
_____

How is the Community involved? How can they be further involved?
_____
_____
_____

What is the Social Enterprise communications strategy? How can it be improved?
_____
_____
_____

What is the marketing strategy?
_____
_____
_____

Describe how revenue is generated.
_____
_____
_____

© Karen Young. 2012.

NOTES

Are there additional ways to generate revenue that fit within the scope of business activity? (Detail)

_____

_____

_____

_____

_____

NOTES

New Enterprise

Use this checklist as a tool for assessing the nature of a prospective social enterprise.
Describe the concept

_____

_____

_____

_____

❑ YES ❑ NO Is this a fit with the Mandate and activities of the nonprofit Organization?
❑ YES ❑ NO Is there a need for this product or service? Do people pay for it now?
❑ YES ❑ NO Who else offers the same or a similar product or service? If no one, why?

_____

_____

❑ YES ❑ NO Is supply for raw materials or wholesale product readily available?

Please describe the product cycle. Will customers purchase this product (choose one)
❑ one time only ❑ 10 years ❑ 2 years ❑ each year ❑ monthly ❑ more often

Please describe the sales environment
❑ Retail storefront ❑ Office ❑ Online ❑ Network ❑ Factory ❑ Other _____

Provide a financial analysis.

Include startup costs. Operating costs. Projected return.

Description	Expense $	Income $	Net $

Based on the information above

Recommendation to Proceed   ❑ Yes   ❑ No

© Karen Young. 2012.

ADDITIONAL THOUGHTS (optional)

_____
_____
_____
_____
_____
_____
_____
_____

Intern Name	Date
Attendance	Engagement
COMMENTS	
Supervisor Name	Supervisor Signature

Excerpt from *The Fundraising Primer*

PREFACE

There are over 80,000 Nonprofit Organizations in Canada and more than 1.2 million in the United States. They range in size from small grassroots Organizations that are operated by a very few volunteers to large and well established Charities employing many hundreds of people.

Their Mandates include social and human services, education, health, religion, those that focus on improving the environment, as well as those promoting arts, sport, heritage and many more.

While there is great need for the services provided by these Nonprofits, in challenging economic times there are decreased funds available to them. They compete for the same philanthropic dollars in order to exist.

Additionally, Organizations struggle to find ways to create sustainable revenue streams for Programs. Boards of Directors and volunteers who are passionate and knowledgeable about the work of the Organization may be unskilled at finding money, at developing resources. There may be anxiety or fear at the thought of having to raise funds, even though the survival of the Organization—and the benefits provided to the Community—depend on sustainable cash flows. But there is good news! There are established, tried-and-true ways to raise funds.

• •

Fundraising can be fun
Fundraising is both rewarding and enjoyable, an opportunity to fully use and develop your skills and interests while contributing to community.
For example:
- Do you love to connect with people and build relationships? *You may love to work directly with donors and get to know them.*
- Do you love to do research and write detailed reports? *You may look forward to writing Grant applications and responding to RFPs (Request for Proposal).*
- Perhaps you love to provide a fun atmosphere that brings happy people together? *You may want to plan informational or fundraising events.*
- Are you creative? *You may enjoy the communications and public relations tasks.*
- Are you are a big-picture visionary? *You may wish to lead a team of fundraisers.*

Find the niche that best suits you. Most professionals become knowledgeable about the broad range of opportunities, and then specialize.

Made in the USA
Charleston, SC
30 September 2012